I0162350

100+
INSPIRATIONAL
Poems and Prose
ABOUT
LIFE *and* SUCCESS

Thought-provoking and Empowering
Words to Uplift and Inspire You

VERUSHA ROBBINS | VIREND SINGH

Copyright 2025 by Verusha Robbins and Virend Singh

All rights reserved. No part of this book may be used or reproduced in any manner whatsoever without written permission from the publisher; exceptions are made for brief quotations embodied in articles and reviews. Your support of the authors' rights is sincerely appreciated.

Published by
Ink 'n Ivory
P O Box 6321, Rouse Hill, NSW. 2155. Australia

www.inkNivory.com
Blog: www.CoolSelfHelpTips.com

First Printing: 2025

ISBN: 978-1-922113-43-6 (Paperback)
ISBN: 978-1-922113-44-3 (ePub)
ISBN: 978-1-922113-45-0 (Hardcover)

Disclaimer

This publication is shared with the understanding that the publisher and author are not engaged in rendering financial, psychological or any other professional service and are offered for information purposes only. If financial or any other professional advice or assistance is required, the services of a competent professional person should be sought. The reader is solely responsible for his/her own actions arising from the use of this document.

A Quick Tip to Maximize Your Learning

Unlock the Full Potential of "100+ Inspirational Poems and Prose About Life and Success."

As you embark on this journey to enrich your life through these life-changing stories, I want to share a life hack I found years ago.

While reading this book, I highly recommend pairing it with the audiobook version. By listening to the audiobook alongside this book, you'll be able to:

- Absorb the material more efficiently
- Retain more information
- Apply the principles to your life more effectively
- Experience a more immersive and engaging learning experience

To get started, secure your copy of the audiobook version of "100+ Inspirational Poems and Prose About Life and Success" from the options provided at the following link:

https://Chosen4U.com/PPAudio/

A Free Gift

A dad-and-daughter initiative to empower individuals to unlock their full potential and achieve their most extraordinary lives with the "hidden" laws of success and happiness.

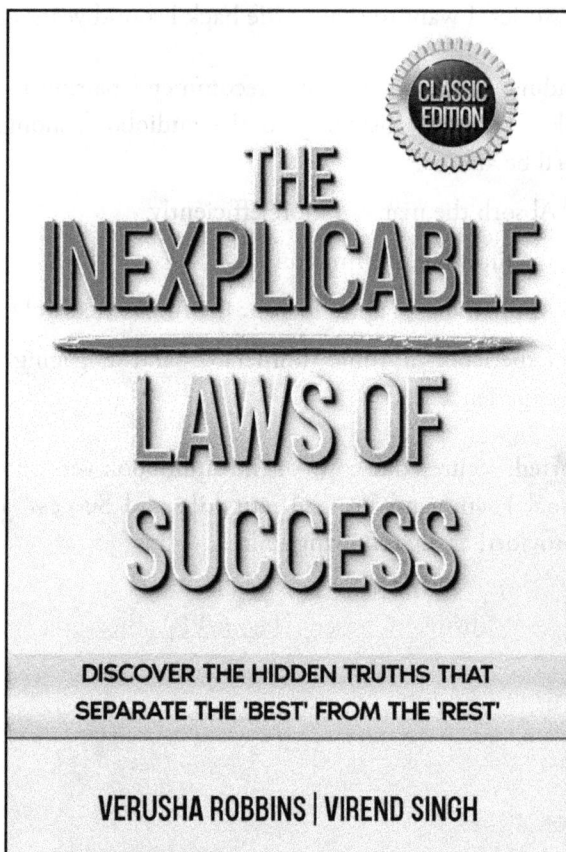

CLASSIC EDITION

THE INEXPLICABLE LAWS OF SUCCESS

DISCOVER THE HIDDEN TRUTHS THAT SEPARATE THE 'BEST' FROM THE 'REST'

VERUSHA ROBBINS | VIREND SINGH

Download from leading online bookstores:
www.Chosen4U.com/tpp

Introduction

Inspiration comes in many forms – goals, nature, music, children, quotes, movies, speeches, art and poetry, to name a few. However, the root of all inspiration is the idea that our lives are meaningful. Inspiration is knowing that what I do matters deeply to the universe. When you have the feeling that your actions are meaningful, you will become filled with strength and vigor to fulfill your life's purpose.

Inspirational content (such as poems, short stories and quotes) enable us to see the world in new ways, whether offering hope for a better future, speaking of faith in a loving god or depicting the beauty of nature and the innate goodness of mankind. They can spur us to achieve great things, or persuade us that we can make it, or encourage us to think big and be ambitious.

The profound poems and prose in this book will touch your heart and inspire you to open to your deeper potential in life. We hope that you find the content absolutely life-changing… so much so that you will download our free puclication "The 10 Best Motivational Stories to Uplift and Inspire" at www.Chosen4u.com/SS10.

Handwriting On The Wall

A weary mother returned from the store,
Lugging groceries through the kitchen door.
Awaiting her arrival was her 8-year-old son,
Anxious to relate what his younger brother had done.

While I was out playing and Dad was on a call,
T.J. took his crayons and wrote on the wall
It's on the new paper you just hung in the den.
I told him you'd be mad at having to do it again.

She let out a moan and furrowed her brow,
Where is your little brother right now?
She emptied her arms and with a purposeful stride,
She marched to his closet where he had gone to hide.

She called his full name as she entered his room.
He trembled with fear--he knew that meant doom
For the next ten minutes, she ranted and raved
About the expensive wallpaper and how she had saved.

Lamenting all the work it would take to repair,
She condemned his actions and total lack of care.
The more she scolded, the madder she got,
Then stomped from his room, totally distraught.

She headed for the den to confirm her fears.
When she saw the wall, her eyes flooded with tears.
The message she read pierced her soul with a dart.
It said, I love Mommy, surrounded by a heart.

Well, the wallpaper remained, just as she found it,
With an empty picture frame hung to surround it.
A reminder to her, and indeed to all,
Take time to read the handwriting on the wall.

~ Unknown

It is in loving, not in being loved
The heart finds its quest
It is in giving, not in getting
Our lives are blest.

~ Unknown

The Little Red Hen

Said the big white rooster, 'Gosh all Hemlock, things are tough,
Seems that worms are getting scarce and I cannot find enough.
What's become of all those fat ones is a mystery to me;
There were thousands through the rainy spell, but now where
can they be?'

The little red hen, who heard him, didn't grumble or complain,
She had been through lots of dry spells, she had lived through
floods of rain;
So she flew up on the grindstone and she gave her claws a whet,
And she said, I've never seen a time there were no worms to get.

She picked a new and undug spot; the earth was hard and firm.
The big white rooster jeered, 'New ground! That's no place for a
worm.'
The little red hen spread her feet, she dug fast and free,
'I must go to the worms,' she said, 'the worms won't come to
me.'

The rooster vainly spent his day, through habit by the ways,
Where fat worms have passed in squads, back in the rainy days.
When nightfall found him supperless, he growled in accents
rough,
'I'm as hungry as a fowl can be. Conditions sure are tough.'

He turned to the little red hen and said, 'It's worse with you,
For you're not only hungry, but you must be tired too.
I rested while I watched for worms, so I feel fairly perk;
But how are you? Without worms, too? And after all that work?

The little red hen hopped to her perch and dropped her eyes to sleep,
And murmured, in a drowsy tone, 'Young man, hear this and weep,
I'm full of worms and happy, for I've dined both long and well,
The worms were there, as always, but I had to dig like hell!'

Oh, here and there white roosters are still holding sales positions,
They cannot do much business now, because of poor conditions.
But as soon as things get right again, they'll sell a hundred firms,
Meanwhile, the little red hens are out, a-gobbling up the worms.

~ Anonymous

Luck

He worked by day, and toiled by night,
He gave up play and some delight,
Dry books he read, new things to learn!
And forged ahead, success to earn,
He plodded on with faith and pluck.
And when he won, men called it Luck.

-Anonymous

Forgive Me When I Whine

Today, upon a bus,
I saw a lovely girl with golden hair.
I envied her. She seemed so happy;
I wished I were as fair.

When suddenly she rose to leave,
I saw her hobble down the aisle;
She had one leg and wore a crutch;
But as she passed...a smile!

Oh, God forgive me when I whine,
I have two legs. The world is mine!

I stopped to buy some candy.
The lad who sold it had such charm.
I talked with him.
He seemed so glad.
If I were late, it would do no harm.
And as I left, he said to me,
"I thank you; You have been so kind.
It's nice to talk with folks like you.
You see," he said, "I'm blind."

Oh, God forgive me when I whine,
I have two eyes. The world is mine!

Later, while walking down the street,
I saw a child with eyes of blue.
He stood and watched the others play.
He did not know what to do.
I stopped a moment; then I said,
'Why don't you join the others, dear?'
He looked ahead without a word,
and then I knew he could not hear.
Oh, God forgive me when I whine,
I have two ears.
The world is mine!

With feet to take me where I'd go,
with eyes to see the sunset's glow,
with ears to hear what I would know...
Oh, God forgive me when I whine.
I'm blessed indeed.
The world is mine!

~ Red Foley

The Hustling Pumpkin Vine

Say boy, don't go a mopin' 'round 'n' talkin' in a whine,
But go out in the field and view the hustling pumpkin vine.
It has the kind o' stuff in it that's needed, boy, in you,
A kind o' gets there quality that most folks say will do.

The weeds may grow around it but the pumpkin vine don't stop,
It shows it's there fer business an' it climbs right out on top.
An' if it strikes a big stone fence or ditch that may be wide,

It jes' lines out 'n strings the pumpkins on the other side.
So boy, don't let the weeds or ditches drive you from your way,
But go ahead and get on top—do something every day.
An' if things look discouraging, don't ever mope or whine,
But go and learn a lesson from the hustling pumpkin vine.

~ Ed Blair

<hr>

Faith, mighty faith
The promise sees
And looks to God alone,
Laughs at impossibilities
And cries, 'It shall be done.'

~ Unknown

Unique

Because I know who I am,
I'm at ease and free.
I can't be like others,
And they can't be me.

I've got fading scars,
An unusual physique,
But it all works together
To make me unique.

I've got hidden strengths,
Some obvious flaws.
Still, I am who I am,
For better, for worse.

I don't have to blend in;
I won't live a lie.
I can't please everyone;
I won't even try.

Some call me proud;
Others stare at me in alarm.
But I'm not one to bother,
Because I know who I am.

~ Abimbola T. Alabi

"Now" & "Waitawhile"

Little Jimmie "Waitawhile" and little Johnnie "Now"
Grew up in homes just side by side; and that, you see, is how
I came to know them both so well, for almost every day
I used to watch them in their work and also in their play.

Little Jimmie "Waitawhile" was bright and steady, too,
But never ready to perform what he was asked to do;
"Wait just a minute," he would say, "I'll do it pretty soon,"
And tasks he should have done at morn were never done at
noon.

He put off studying until his boyhood days were gone;
He put off getting him a home till age came stealing on;
He put off everything, and so his life was not a joy,
And all because he waited "just a minute" when a boy.

But little Johnnie "Now" would say, when he had work to do,
"There's no time like the present time," and gaily put it through.
And when his time for play arrived, he so enjoyed the fun!
His mind was not distressed with thoughts of duties left undone.

In boyhood he was studious and laid him out a plan
Of action to be followed when he grew to be a man;
And life was as he willed it, all because he'd not allow
His tasks to be neglected, but would always do them "now."

And so in every neighborhood are scores of growing boys
Who, by and by, must work with tools when they have done
with toys.
And you know one of them, I guess, because I see you smile;
And is he little Johnnie "Now" or Jimmie "Waitawhile"?

~ Nixon Waterman

Whose Job Is It?

Everybody, Somebody, Anybody, and Nobody were members of a group.
There was an important job to do and Everybody was asked to do it.
Everybody was sure that Somebody would do it.
Anybody would have done it, but Nobody did it.
Somebody got angry because it was Everybody's job.
Everybody thought Anybody would do it, but Nobody realized that Anybody wouldn't do it.
It ended up that Everybody, blamed Somebody, when Nobody did, what Anybody could have done.

~ Adapted from poem by Charles Osgood

No Vision and you perish;
No Ideal, and you're last;
Your heart must ever Cherish,
Some Faith at any cost.
Some hope, some Dream to cling to,
Some Rainbow in the sky,
Some Melody to sing to,
Some Service that is high.

~ Harriet Du Autermont

The Little Chap Who Follows Me

A careful man I want to be;
A little fellow follows me.
I do not dare to go astray
For fear he'll go the self-same way.

I cannot once escape his eyes,
Whate'er he sees me do, he tries.
Like me he says he's going to be;
The little chap who follows me.

He thinks that I'm so very fi ne,
Believes in every word of mine.
The base in me he must not see;
The little chap who follows me.

I must remember as I go
Through summer's sun and winter's snow,
I'm building for the years to be;
The little chap who follows me.

~ Unknown

Lessons From An Oyster

There once was an oyster
Whose story I tell,
Who found that some sand
Had got into his shell.

It was only a grain,
but it gave him great pain.
For oysters have feelings
Although they're so plain.

Now, did he berate
the harsh workings of fate
That had brought him
To such a deplorable state?

Did he curse at the government,
Cry for election,
And claim that the sea should
Have given him protection?

'No,' he said to himself
As he lay on a shell,
Since I cannot remove it,
I shall try to improve it.

Now the years have rolled around,
As the years always do,
And he came to his ultimate
Destiny stew.

And the small grain of sand
That had bothered him so
Was a beautiful pearl
All richly aglow.

Now the tale has a moral,
for isn't it grand
What an oyster can do
With a morsel of sand?

What couldn't we do
If we'd only begin
With some of the things
That get under our skin.

~ Unknown

Only as high as I reach can I grow,
only as far as I seek can I go,
only as deep as I look can I see,
only as much as I dream can I be.

~ Karen Ravn

It Couldn't be Done

Somebody said that it couldn't be done,
But, he with a chuckle replied
That "maybe it couldn't" but he would be one
Who wouldn't say so till he'd tried.

So he buckled right in with the trace of a grin
On his face. If he worried, he hid it.
He started to sing as he tackled the thing
That couldn't be done, as he did it.

Somebody scoffed: "Oh, you'll never do that;
At least no one we know has done it";
But he took off his coat and he took off his hat,
And the first thing we knew he'd begun it.

With a lift of his chin and a bit of a grin,
Without any doubting or quiddit,
He started to sing as he tackled the thing
That couldn't be done, and he did it.

There are thousands to tell you it cannot be done,
There are thousands to prophesy failure;
There are thousands to point out to you, one by one,
The dangers that wait to assail you.

But just buckle right in with a bit of a grin,
Just take off your coat and go to it;
Just start to sing as you tackle the thing
That cannot be done, and you'll do it

- Edgar Guest

You Tell On Yourself

You tell what you are by the friends you seek,
By the very manner in which you speak,
By the way you employ your leisure time,
By the use you make of dollar and dime.

You tell what you are by the things you wear,
By the spirit in which you burdens bear,
By the kind of things at which you laugh,
By records you play on the phonograph.

You tell what you are by the way you walk,
By the things of which you delight to talk,
By the manner in which you bear defeat,
By so simple a thing as how you eat.

By the books you choose from the well-filled shelf;
In these ways, and more, you tell on yourself.

~ Unknown

Not what we give, but what we share,
For the gift without the giver is bare.

~ James Russell Lowell

Dancing With God

When I meditated on the word Guidance,
I kept seeing 'dance' at the end of the word.

I remember reading that doing God's will is a lot like dancing.
When two people try to lead, nothing feels right.
The movement doesn't flow with the music,
and everything is quite uncomfortable and jerky.

When one person realizes that, and lets the other lead, both
bodies begin to flow with the music.
One gives gentle cues, perhaps with a nudge to the back or by
pressing lightly in one direction or another.
It's as if two become one body, moving beautifully.

The dance takes surrender, willingness,
and attentiveness from one person
and gentle guidance and skill from the other.

My eyes drew back to the word Guidance.
When I saw 'G': I thought of God, followed by 'u' and 'i'.
'God, 'u' and 'i' dance.'
God, you, and I dance.

~ Unknown

The Time Is Now

We have but a short time
On this earth,
So, value your life
For what it's really worth.
Your life has purpose.
God sent you on a mission.
To live, to love, to learn –
Is His commission.

The world needs you.
Believe me, it's true!
Some things need doing
That only you can do.

Character matters;
Be your own person,
Your own original self,
Not someone else's version.

Develop your talents;
They are unique.
Use your time well;
Listen only to positive critique.

Go after your dreams.
Be bold. Be brave.
Swim against the stream;
It's more than okay.

The time is now
To find your passion.
Time waits for no one,
So, get into action.

To be free of regret
In your old age,
Never ever forget
To fully live today!

~ Bettina Van Vaerenbergh

I Am

I know not whence I came,
I know not whither I go;
But the fact stands clear that I am here
In this world of pleasure and woe.
And out of the mist and murk
Another truth shines plain –
It is my power each day and hour
To add to its joy or its pain.

~ Ella Wheeler Wilcox

Don't Quit

When things go wrong as they sometimes will,
When the road you're trudging seems all uphill.
When the funds are low and the debts are high,
And you want to smile, but you have to sigh.
When care is pressing you down a bit,
Rest if you must, but don't you quit.

Life is queer with its twists and turns,
As every one of us sometimes learns.
And many a fellow turns about,
When he might have won had he stuck it out.
Don't give up though the pace seems slow,
You may succeed with another blow.

Often the goal is nearer than
It seems to a faint and faltering man.
Often the struggler has given up,
When he might have captured the victor's cup.
And he learned too late when the night came down,
How close he was to the golden crown.

Success is failure turned inside out,
The silver tint of the clouds of doubt.
And you never can tell how close you are,
It may be near when it seems afar.
So stick to the fight when you're hardest hit,
It's when things seem worst that you mustn't quit.

~ Unknown

Effort

He brought me his report card from the teacher and he said
He wasn't very proud of it and sadly bowed his head.
He was excellent in reading, but arithmetic, was fair,
And I noticed there were several "unsatisfactory" there;

But one little bit of credit which was given brought me joy—
He was "excellent in effort," and I fairly hugged the boy.
"Oh, it doesn't make much difference what is written on your card,"
I told that little fellow, "if you're only trying hard.

The 'very goods' and 'excellent' are fine, I must agree,
But the effort you are making means a whole lot more to me;
And the thing that's most important when this card is put aside
Is to know, in spite of failure, that to do your best you've tried.

"Just keep excellent in effort—all the rest will come to you.
There isn't any problem but some day you'll learn to do,
And at last, when you grow older, you will come to understand
That by hard and patient toiling men have risen to command

And some day you will discover when a greater goals at stake
That better far than brilliance is the effort you will make."

~ Edgar A. Guest

I Choose The Mountain

The low lands call
I am tempted to answer
They are offering me a free dwelling
Without having to conquer

The massive mountain makes its move
Beckoning me to ascend
A much more difficult path
To get up the slippery bend

I cannot choose both
I have a choice to make
I must be wise
This will determine my fate

I choose, I choose the mountain
With all its stress and strain
Because only by climbing
Can I rise above the plane

I choose the mountain
And I will never stop climbing
I choose the mountain
And I shall forever be ascending

I choose the mountain

~ Howard Simon

We Are What We Think

We are what we think.
All that we are arises with our thoughts.
With our thoughts we make the world.
Speak or act with an impure mind
And trouble will follow you
As the wheel follows the ox that draws the cart.

We are what we think.
All that we are arises with our thoughts.
With our thoughts we make the world.
Speak or act with a pure mind
And happiness will follow you
As your shadow, unbreakable.

How can a troubled mind
Understand the way?

Your worst enemy cannot harm you
As much as your own thoughts, unguarded.

But once mastered,
No one can help you as much,
Not even your father or your mother.

~ Dhammapada, The Buddha

Prayer

I asked for strength and
God gave me difficulties to make me strong

I asked for wisdom and
God gave me problems to solve

I asked for prosperity and
God gave me brawn and brains to work

I asked for courage and
God gave me dangers to overcome

I asked for patience and
God placed me in situations where I was forced to wait

I asked for love and
God gave me troubled people to help

I asked for favors and
God gave me opportunities

I received nothing I wanted
I received everything I needed

My Prayer Has Been Answered

~ Unknown

My Wage

I bargained with Life for a penny,
And Life would pay no more,
However I begged at evening
When I counted my scanty store;

For Life is a just employer,
He gives you what you ask,
But once you have set the wages,
Why, you must bear the task.

I worked for a menial's hire,
Only to learn, dismayed,
That any wage I had asked of Life,
Life would have gladly paid.

~ Jessie B Rittenhouse

I slept and dreamt that life was joy
I awoke and found that life was
duty
I acted, and behold!
Duty was joy.

~ Rabindranath Tagore

Thinking

If you think you are beaten, you are
If you think you dare not, you don't,
If you like to win, but you think you can't
It is almost certain you won't.

If you think you'll lose, you've lost
For out of the world we find,
Success begins with a fellow's will
It's all in the state of mind.

If you think you are outclassed, you are
You've got to think high to rise,
You've got to be sure of yourself before
You can ever win a prize.

Life's battles don't always go
To the stronger or faster man,
But soon or late the man who wins
Is the man WHO THINKS HE CAN!

~ Walter D. Wintle

Victory

You are the Man who used to boast
That you'd achieve the uttermost,
Some day.

You merely wished to show,
To demonstrate how much you know
And prove the distance you can go.

Another year we've just passed through.
What new ideas came to you?
How many big things did you do?

Time left twelve fresh months in your care
How many of them did you share
With opportunity and dare
Again where you so often missed?

We do not find you on the list of makers good.
Explain the fact!
Ah No, 'Twas not the chance you lacked!
As usual - you failed to act!

~ Herbert Kauffman

The Laggard's Excuse

He worked by day
And toiled by night,
He gave up play
And some delight.
Dry books he read
New things to learn
And forged ahead,
Success to earn.
He plodded on
With faith and pluck,
And when he won
Men called it luck.

~ Unknown

M. Guffey's Primer

Work while you work,
Play while you play;
One thing each time,
That is the way.
All that you do,
Do with your might;
Things done by halves
Are not done right!

~ Unknown

The Indispensable Man

Sometimes, when you're feeling important,
Sometimes, when your ego's in bloom,
Sometimes, when you take it for granted
You're the best qualified in the room.

Sometimes, when you feel that your going
Would leave an unfilled hole,
Just follow this simple instruction,
and see how it humbles your soul:

Take a bucket and fill it with water,
Put your hand in it up to the wrist,
Pull it out and the hole that's remaining
Is a measure of how you'll be missed.

You may splash all you please when you enter,
You can stir up the water galore,
But stop, and you'll find in a minute
That it looks quite the same as before.

The moral of this quaint example
Is to do just the best that you can;
Be proud of yourself, but remember,
There is no indispensable man. (or woman)

~ Saxon White Kessinger

Stick To Your Job

Diamonds are only chunks of coal
That stuck to their jobs, you see;
If they'd petered out, as most of us do,
Where would the diamonds be?
It isn't the fact of making a start,
It's the sticking that counts, I'll say;
It's the fellow that knows not the meaning of fail,
But hammers and hammers away.
Whenever you think that you've come to the end,
And you're beaten as bad as can be,
Remember that diamonds are chunks of coal
That stuck to their jobs you see.

~ Minnie Richard Smith

Even after all this time,
The Sun never says to the earth:
"You owe me!"
Look at what happens with,
A love like that!
It lights the whole sky!

~ Hafiz

Cookie Thief

A woman was waiting at an airport one night,
With several long hours before her flight.
She hunted for a book in the airport shops.
Bought a bag of cookies and found a place to drop.

She was engrossed in her book but happened to see,
That the man sitting beside her, as bold as could be.
Grabbed a cookie or two from the bag in between,
Which she tried to ignore to avoid a scene.

So she munched the cookies and watched the clock,
As the gutsy cookie thief diminished her stock.
She was getting more irritated as the minutes ticked by,
Thinking, "If I wasn't so nice, I would blacken his eye."

With each cookie she took, he took one too,
When only one was left, she wondered what he would do.
With a smile on his face, and a nervous laugh,
He took the last cookie and broke it in half.

He offered her half, as he ate the other,
She snatched it from him and thought... oooh, brother.
This guy has some nerve and he's also rude,
Why he didn't even show any gratitude!

She had never known when she had been so galled,
And sighed with relief when her flight was called.
She gathered her belongings and headed to the gate,
Refusing to look back at the thieving ingrate.

She boarded the plane, and sank in her seat,
Then she sought her book, which was almost complete.
As she reached in her baggage, she gasped with surprise,
There was her bag of cookies, in front of her eyes.

If mine are here, she moaned in despair,
The others were his, and he tried to share.
Too late to apologize, she realized with grief,
That she was the rude one, the ingrate, the thief.

~ Valerie Cox

If there is light in the soul,
There will be beauty in the person.
If there is beauty in the person,
There will be harmony in the house.
If there is harmony in the house,
There will be order in the nation.
If there is order in the nation,
There will be peace in the world.

~ Chinese Proverb

The Bridge Builder

An old man, going a lone highway,
Came, at the evening, cold and gray,
To a chasm, vast, and deep, and wide,
Through which was flowing a sullen tide.
The old man crossed in the twilight dim;
The sullen stream had no fears for him;
But he turned, when safe on the other side,
And built a bridge to span the tide.

"Old man", said a fellow pilgrim, near,
"You are wasting strength with building here;
Your journey will end with the ending day;
You never again will pass this way;
You've crossed the chasm, deep and wide, —
Why build you this bridge at the eventide?"

The builder lifted his old gray head:
"Good friend, in the path I have come", he said,
"There followed after me to-day
A youth, whose feet must pass this way.
This chasm, that has been naught to me,
To that fair-haired youth may a pitfall be.
He, too, must cross in the twilight dim;
Good friend, I am building this bridge for him."

~ Will Allen Dromgoole (1860-1934)

Entrepreneur's Credo

I do not choose to be a common man,
It is my right to be uncommon … if I can,
I seek opportunity … not security.

I do not wish to be a kept citizen.
Humbled and dulled by having the
State look after me.

I want to take the calculated risk;
To dream and to build.
To fail and to succeed.

I refuse to barter incentive for a dole;
I prefer the challenges of life
To the guaranteed existence;
The thrill of fulfillment
To the stale calm of Utopia.

I will not trade freedom for beneficence
Nor my dignity for a handout
I will never cower before any master
Nor bend to any threat.

It is my heritage to stand erect.
Proud and unafraid;
To think and act for myself,
To enjoy the benefit of my creations
And to face the world boldly and say:
This, with God's help, I have done.

All this is what it means
To be an Entrepreneur.

~ Thomas Paine, Author of *"Common Sense"*

---◆○◆---

Challenges of Life

Smooth roads never make good drivers
Smooth seas never make good sailors
Clear skies never makes good pilots.
Problem-free life never makes a strong person
Be strong enough to accept the challenges of Life
Don't ask Life, "Why Me?"
Instead, say "Try Me!"

~ Unknown

Leisure

What is this life if, full of care,
We have no time to stand and stare.

No time to stand beneath the boughs
And stare as long as sheep or cows.

No time to see, when woods we pass,
Where squirrels hide their nuts in grass.

No time to see, in broad daylight,
Streams full of stars, like skies at night.

No time to turn at Beauty's glance,
And watch her feet, how they can dance.

No time to wait till her mouth can
Enrich that smile her eyes began.

A poor life this if, full of care,
We have no time to stand and stare.

- W H Davies

Little Eyes Upon You

There are little eyes upon you,
And they are watching night and day;
There are little ears that quickly
Take in every word you say.
There are little hands all eager
To do everything you do;
and a little boy who's dreaming
Of the day he'll be like you.
You're the little fellow's idol;
You're the wisest of the wise;
In his little mind, about you
No suspicions ever rise.

He believes in you devotedly,
Holds that all you say and do,
He will say and do in your way
When he's grown up like you.
There's a wide-eyed little fellow
Who believes you're always right;
And his ears are always open,
And he watches day and night.
You are setting an example
Every day in all you do;
For the little boy who's waiting
To grow up to be just like you.

- Author Unknown

Opportunity

With doubt and dismay you are smitten
You think there's no chance for you, son?
Why, the best books haven't been written
The best race hasn't been run,
The best score hasn't been made yet,
The best song hasn't been sung,
The best tune hasn't been played yet,
Cheer up, for the world is young!
No chance? Why the world is just eager
For things that you ought to create
Its store of true wealth is still meagre
Its needs are incessant and great,
It yearns for more power and beauty
More laughter and love and romance,
More loyalty, labor and duty,
No chance – why there's nothing but chance!
For the best verse hasn't been rhymed yet,
The best house hasn't been planned,
The highest peak hasn't been climbed yet,
The mightiest rivers aren't spanned,
Don't worry and fret, faint hearted,
The chances have just begun,
For the Best jobs haven't been started,
The Best work hasn't been done.

~ Berton Braley

Keep-A-Trying

Say "I will!" and then stick to it–
That's the only way to do it.
Don't build up a while and then
Tear the whole thing down again.
Fix the goal you wish to gain,
Then go at it heart and brain,
And, though clouds shut out the blue,
Do not dim your purpose true
With your sighing.
Stand erect, and, like a man,
Know "They can, who think they can!"
Keep a-trying.

Had Columbus, half seas o'er,
Turned back to his native shore,
Men would not, to-day, proclaim
Round the world his deathless name.
So must we sail on with him
Past horizons far and dim,
Till at last we own the prize
That belongs to him who tries
With faith undying;
Own the prize that all may win
Who, with hope, through thick and thin
Keep a-trying.

~ Nixon Waterman

Teamwork

It's all very well to have courage and skill
And it's fine to be counted a star,
But the single deed with its touch of thrill
Doesn't tell the man you are;
For there's no lone hand in the game we play,
We must work to a bigger scheme,
And the thing that counts in the world to-day
Is, How do you pull with the team?

They may sound your praise and call you great,
They may single you out for fame,
But you must work with your running mate
Or you'll never win the game;
Oh, never the work of life is done
By the man with a selfish dream,
For the battle is lost or the battle is won
By the spirit of the team.

You may think it fine to be praised for skill,
But a greater thing to do
Is to set your mind and set your will
On the goal that's just in view;
It's helping your fellowman to score
When his chances hopeless seem;
Its forgetting self till the game is o're
And fighting for the team.

~ Edgar Albert Guest

Risk

To laugh is to risk appearing a fool,
To weep is to risk appearing sentimental.
To reach out to another is to risk involvement,
To expose feelings is to risk exposing your true self.
To place your ideas and dreams before a crowd is to risk their loss
To love is to risk not being loved in return,
To hope is to risk despair,
To try is to risk failure.

But risks must be taken because
the greatest hazard in life is to risk nothing.
The person who risks nothing,
does nothing, has nothing, is nothing.
He may avoid suffering and sorrow,
But he cannot learn, feel, change, grow or live.
Chained by his servitude he is a slave
who has forfeited all freedom.
Only a person who risks is free.

~ William Arthur Ward

Finding A Will When Wanting to Quit

Times will get rough and sometimes tough,
Where you may say that you have had enough,
Where you may fall and need a lift,
Where the hurt of your pains may leave you stiff.

When all things may seem to go wrong,
Just pick up some faith and carry on,
Because you may never know how close you've come to be,
To reach the throne of victory.

There has been some time that passed,
That many thought they could not last.
But with a mighty blow they've come to see,
That they had made history.

When you may feel that there is nothing that you can do,
Here is something you can refer to.
As some people say, "Where there is a will, there's a way."
With this being said, I feel a brighter day,

One without hurt, one without sorrow,
One with a brighter tomorrow.
So, in the fight, you may get knocked down,
But get back up without a frown,

Because it's when you're hardest hit
That you must say that you will not quit.
So, push on harder and hear me when I say,
"Where there's a will, there's a way."

~ Tyquan L. Norwood

God Will Count Your Honest Try

If in life's great, onward battle
You have done your best and lost,
If amid the din and rattle
You regarded not the cost,

If you met your foeman bravely,
If you dared to do or die,
God will credit you, most surely,
For your fearless, honest try.

Have you sometimes felt discouraged?
Felt that life had lost its charm,
And that every effort failed you,
Bringing to you only harm?

Look within and ask this question:
"Have I done my level best?"
If you answer, without guessing,
"Yes," then God will do the rest.

Has this neighbor won more glory?
That one more of earthly store?
Though your hair is thin and hoary,
Are you poorer than before?

Have you helped, with hands quite willing?
Have you heard the orphan's cry?
Given part of your last shilling?
God will count your honest try.

~ William Henry Dawson

Good Timber

The tree that never had to fight
For sun and sky and air and light,
But stood out in the open plain
And always got its share of rain,
Never became a forest king
But lived and died a scrubby thing.

The man who never had to toil
To gain and farm his patch of soil,
Who never had to win his share?
Of sun and sky and light and air,
Never became a manly man
But lived and died as he began.

Good timber does not grow with ease,
The stronger wind, the stronger trees,
The further sky, the greater length,
The more the storm, the more the strength.
By sun and cold, by rain and snow,
In trees and men good timbers grow.

Where thickest lies the forest growth
We find the patriarchs of both.
And they hold counsel with the stars
Whose broken branches show the scars
Of many winds and much of strife.
This is the common law of life.

~ Douglas Malloch

Compensation

I'd like to think when life is done
That I had filled a needed post.
That here and there I'd paid my fare
With more than idle talk and boast;
That I had taken gifts divine.
The breath of life and manhood fine,
And tried to use them now and then
In service for my fellow men.

I'd hate to think when life is through
That I had lived my round of years
A useless kind, that leaves behind
No record in this vale of tears;
That I had wasted all my days
By treading only selfish ways,
And that this world would be the same
If it had never known my name.

I'd like to think that here and there,
When I am gone, there shall remain
A happier spot that might have not
Existed had I toiled for gain;
That someone's cheery voice and smile
Shall prove that I had been worth while;
That I had paid with something fine
My debt to God for life divine.

~ Edgar Albert Guest

Climb 'Til Your Dream Comes True

Often your tasks will be many,
And more than you think you can do.
Often the road will be rugged
And the hills insurmountable, too.

But always remember, the hills ahead
Are never as steep as they seem,
And with Faith in your heart start upward
And climb 'Til you reach your dream.

For nothing in life that is worthy
Is never too hard to achieve
If you have the courage to try it
And you have the Faith to believe.

For Faith is a force that is greater
Than knowledge or power or skill
And many defeats turn to triumph
If you trust in God's wisdom and will.

For Faith is a mover of mountains.
There's nothing that God cannot do,
So start out today with Faith in your heart
And 'Climb 'Til Your Dream Comes True'!

~ Helen Steiner Rice

Ideals

Remember that ideals
are like stars up in the sky,
You can never really reach them,
hanging in the heavens high …

But like the mighty mariner
who sailed the storm-tossed sea,
And used the stars to chart his course
with skill and certainty,

You too can chart your course in life
with high ideals and love,
For high ideals are like the stars
that light the sky above …

You cannot ever reach them,
but lift your heart up high
And your life will be as shining
as the stars up in the sky.

~ Helen Steiner Rice

I Bend

I bend but do not break.
I've been lost, but I'm not a loser.
I'm a wreck, but I'm not totaled.
I'm fractured but not broken.
I've failed, but I'm not a failure.
I've fallen hard but can get up again.
I'm isolated, but still I'm free.
I have been destroyed but will rebuild.
My heart is broken, but it will mend.
See, no matter how close I come to breaking,
I just continue to bend.

~ Selena Odom

If I Can Stop One Heart From Breaking

If I can stop one heart from breaking,
I shall not live in vain.
If I can ease one life the aching,
Or cool one pain,
Or help one fainting robin
Unto his nest again,
I shall not live in vain.

~ Emily Dickinson

Promise Yourself

Promise yourself to be so strong that nothing can disturb your peace of mind.

To talk health, happiness, and prosperity to every person you meet.

To make all your friends feel like there is something in them.

To look at the sunny side of everything and make your optimism come true.

To think only of the best, to work only for the best, and expect only the best.

To be just as enthusiastic about the success of others as you are about your own.

To forget the mistakes of the past and press on the greater achievements of the future.

To wear a cheerful countenance at all times and give every living person you meet a smile.

To give so much time to the improvement of yourself that you have no time to criticize others.

To be too large for worry, too noble for anger, and too strong for fear, and too happy to permit the presence of trouble.

~ The Optimist International

A Home Song

I turned an ancient poet's book,
And found upon the page:
"Stone walls do not a prison make,
Nor iron bars a cage."
Yes, that is true, and something more:
You'll find, where'er you roam,
That marble floors and gilded walls
Can never make a home.
But every house where Love abides,
And Friendship is the guest,
Is surely home, and home, sweet home,
For there the heart can rest.

~ Henry van Dyke

If you love a flower, don't pick it up.
Because if you pick it up it dies
and it ceases to be what you love.
So, if you love a flower, let it be.
Love is not about possession.
Love it about appreciation.

~ Osho

Start Where You Stand

"Start where you stand and never mind the past,
The past won't help you in beginning new,
If you have left it all behind at last
Why, that's enough, you're done with it, you're through;
This is another chapter in the book,
This is another race that you have planned,
Don't give the vanished days a backward look,
Start where you stand."

~ Berton Braley

―◆◇◆―

Losing With A Smile

Let others cheer the winning man,
There's one I hold worthwhile;
'Tis he who does the best he can,
Then loses with a smile.

Beaten he is, but not to stay
Down with the rank and file;
That man will win some other day,
Who loses with a smile.

~ Unknown

Of Birth and Rebirth

This breath that comes and goes
These nerves from head to toes
This mind that's never still
Always there to impose its will

This heart beating day & night
This face, often showing my plight
These muscles, strong but fading fast
These eyes & ears that won't last

These cravings daily born anew
These biases, many, most untrue
This hair, here and gone tomorrow
All these, I had to borrow

To experience life in all its glory
To learn through a new story
And when this story of mine is done
I will prepare for another one.

One by one every time
A rung on the ladder, I aim to climb
Sometimes slipping sadly down
When I believe I'm my gown

This will happen again and again
Till this 'I' does not remain
And everything that we can see
Becomes me – just only me

~ Kishore Asthana (https://sanitybalance.in/)

Crabbit Old Woman

Backstory

The story goes that the following poem was found among the personal belongings of an old lady who died in a geriatric ward of a small hospital near Dundee, Scotland. It was believed that she had nothing left of any value. Later, when the nurses were going through her meagre possessions, they found this poem. However, the truth is it was written by a nurse in a Scots geriatric hospital and shot to prominence after being printed in The Post more than 40 years ago. (**Crabbit** is Scots for "bad-tempered" or "grumpy".)

(Sometimes Published as "Look Closer Nurse")

What do you see, nurse, what do you see?
What are you thinking, when you look at me-
A crabbit old woman, not very wise,
Uncertain of habit, with far-away eyes,
Who dribbles her food and makes no reply
When you say in a loud voice, "I do wish you'd try."
Who seems not to notice the things that you do
And forever is losing a stocking or shoe.
Who, unresisting or not; lets you do as you will
With bathing and feeding the long day is fill.
Is that what you're thinking; Is that what you see?
Then open your eyes, nurse, you're looking at me.

I'll tell you who I am as I sit here so still!
As I rise at your bidding, as I eat at your will.
I'm a small child of 10 with a father and mother,
Brothers and sisters, who loved one another-
A young girl of 16 with wings on her feet,
Dreaming that soon now a lover she'll meet,
A bride soon at 20 - my heart gives a leap,
Recalling the vows that I promised to keep.
At 25 now I have young of my own
Who need me to build a secure happy home;

A woman of 30, my young now grow fast,
Bound to each other with ties that should last;
At 40, my young sons have grown and are gone,
But my man is beside me to see I don't mourn;
At 50 once more babies play around my knee,
Again we know children, my loved one and me.

Dark days are upon me, my husband is dead,
I look at the future, I shudder with dread,
For my young are all rearing young ones of their own.
And I think of the years and the love that I've known;
I'm an old woman now and nature is cruel-
Tis her jest to make old age look like a fool.
The body is crumbled, grace and vigor depart,
There is now a stone where I once had a heart,
But inside this old carcass, a young girl still dwells,
And now and again my battered heart swells,
I remember the joy, I remember the pain,
And I'm loving and living life over again.
I think of the years all too few- gone too fast.
And accept the stark fact that nothing can last-
So open your eyes, nurse, open and see,
Not a crabbit old woman, look closer-
See ME.

- By Phyliss McCormick

A Nurse's Reply
(to "Crabbit Old Woman")

What do we see, you ask, what do we see?
Yes, we are thinking when looking at thee!
We may seem to be hard when we hurry and fuss,
But there's many of you, and too few of us.

We would like far more time to sit by you and talk,
To bath you and feed you and help you to walk.
To hear of your lives and the things you have done;
Your childhood, your husband, your daughter, your son.

But time is against us, there's too much to do –
Patients too many, and nurses too few.
We grieve when we see you so sad and alone
With nobody near you, no friends of your own.

We feel all your pain, and know of your fear
That nobody cares now your end is so near

But nurses are people with feelings as well,
And when we're together you'll often hear tell
Of the dearest old Gran in the very end bed,
And the lovely old Dad, and the things that he said,

We speak with compassion and love, and feel sad
When we think of your lives and the joy that you've had,
When the time has arrived for you to depart,
You leave us behind with an ache in our heart.

When you sleep the long sleep, no more worry or care,
There are other old people, and we must be there.
So please understand if we hurry and fuss -
There are many of you, And so few of us.

~ Liz Hogben / Bruni Abbott

Thoughts Are Things

I hold it true that thoughts are things,
They're endowed with bodies and breath and wings:
And that we send them forth to fill
The world with good results, or ill.
That which we call our secret thought
Speeds forth to Earth's remotest spot,
Leaving its blessings or woes
Like tracks behind as it goes.
We build our future, thought by thought,
For good or ill, yet know it not.
Yet so the Universe was wrought.
Thought is another name for fate;
Choose then thy destiny and wait,
For love brings love and hate brings hate.

~ Henry Van Dyke

The Comfort Zone

I used to have a comfort zone where I knew I wouldn't fail.
The same four walls and busywork were really more like jail.
I longed so much to do the things I'd never done before,
But stayed inside my comfort zone and paced the same old floor.

I said it didn't matter that I wasn't doing much.
I said I didn't care for things like commission cheques and such.
I claimed to be so busy with things inside my zone,
But deep inside I longed for something special of my own.

I couldn't let my life go by just watching others win.
I held my breath; I stepped outside and let the change begin.
I took a step and with new strength I'd never felt before,
I kissed my comfort zone goodbye and closed and locked the door.

If you're in a comfort zone, afraid to venture out,
Remember that all winners were at one time filled with doubt.
A step or two and words of praise can make your dreams come true.
Reach for your future with a smile; success is there for you!

~ Anonymous

Be The Best of Whatever You Are

If you can't be a pine on the top of the hill,
Be a scrub in the valley-but be
The best little scrub by the side of the rill;
Be a bush if you can't be a tree.

If you can't be a bush be a bit of the grass,
And some highway happier make;
If you can't be a muskie then just be a bass
But the liveliest bass in the lake!

We can't all be captains, we've got to be crew,
There's something for all of us here,
There's big work to do, and there's lesser to do,
And the task you must do is the near.

If you can't be a highway then just be a trail,
If you can't be the sun, be a star;
It isn't by size that you win or you fail
Be the best of whatever you are!

~ Douglas Malloch

Comparisons

If you've never trod the valley,
    You can never see the heights,
If you've never walked in darkness,
    You'll never see the light,
If you do not climb the hill ahead,
    You can't look round the bend,
If you're never really lonely,
    You'll never need a friend,
If you've never failed, and failed again,
    You'll never try your best,
If you've never suffered sleeplessness,
    You'll never know true rest,
If you've never stumbled through the clouds,
    You'll never see the blue,
If you've never suffered grief or pain,
    Real joy won't come to you,
For the one calls forth the other,
    As onward we must go,
Don't ask me how I found this out,
    Let me just say "I know".

~ Unknown

The Cold Within

Six humans trapped by happenstance
in bleak and bitter cold.
Each one possessed a stick of wood
or so the story's told.

Their dying fire in need of logs
but a white man held his back.
For of the faces round the fire
he noticed one was black.

The next man looking cross the way
saw one not of his church.
And couldn't bring himself to give
the fire his stick of birch.

The third one sat in tattered clothes
he gave his coat a hitch.
Why should his log be put to use
to warm the idle rich?

The rich man just sat back and thought
of the wealth he had in store.
And how to keep what he had earned
from the lazy, shiftless poor.

The black man's face bespoke revenge
as the fire passed from his sight.
For all he saw in his stack of wood
was a chance to spite the white.

The last man of this forlorn group
did naught except for gain.
Giving only to those who gave
was how he played the game.

Their logs held tight in death's still hand
was proof of human sin.
They did not die from the cold outside
they died from the cold within.

~ Jay Patrick Kinney

Help Yourself To Happiness

Everybody, everywhere seeks happiness, it's true,
But finding it and keeping it seem difficult to do.
Difficult because we think that happiness is found
Only in the places where wealth and fame abound.
And so we go on searching in palaces of pleasure
Seeking recognition and monetary treasure,
Unaware that happiness is just a state of mind
Within the reach of everyone who takes time to be kind.
For in making others happy we will be happy, too.
For the happiness you give away returns to shine on you.

~ Helen Steiner Rice

Sermons We See

I'd rather see a sermon
than hear one any day;
I'd rather one should walk with me
than merely tell the way.

The eye's a better pupil
and more willing than the ear,
Fine counsel is confusing,
but example's always clear;

And the best of all the preachers
are the men who live their creeds,
For to see good put in action
is what everybody needs.

I soon can learn to do it
if you'll let me see it done;
I can watch your hands in action,
but your tongue too fast may run.

And the lecture you deliver
may be very wise and true,
But I'd rather get my lessons
by observing what you do;

For I might misunderstand you
and the high advice you give,
But there's no misunderstanding
how you act and how you live.

When I see a deed of kindness,
I am eager to be kind.
When a weaker brother stumbles
and a strong man stays behind

Just to see if he can help him,
then the wish grows strong in me
To become as big and thoughtful
as I know that friend to be.

And all travelers can witness
that the best of guides today
Is not the one who tells them,
but the one who shows the way.

One good man teaches many,
men believe what they behold;
One deed of kindness noticed
is worth forty that are told.

Who stands with men of honor
learns to hold his honor dear,
For right living speaks a language
which to everyone is clear.

Though an able speaker charms me
with his eloquence, I say,
I'd rather see a sermon
than to hear one, any day.

~ Edgar A. Guest

The Invitation

It doesn't interest me what you do for a living; I want to know what you ache for and if you dare to dream of meeting your hearts longing.

It doesn't interest me how old you are, I want to know if you will risk looking like a fool for love, for your dream, for the adventure of being alive.

It doesn't interest me what planets are squaring your moon, I want to know if you have touched the center of your sorrow, if you have been opened by life's betrayals or have become shriveled and closed from fear of further pain.

I want to know if you can sit with pain, mine or your own; without moving to hide it or fade it, or fix it. I want to know if you can be with joy mine or your own; and if you can dance with wildness and let the ecstasy fill you to the tips of your fingers and toes without cautioning us to be careful, be realistic, or to remember the limitations of being human.

It doesn't interest me if the story you are telling me is true, I want to know if you can disappoint another to be true to yourself, if you can bear the accusation of betrayal and not betray your own soul.

I want to know if you can be faithful and therefore trustworthy, I want to know if you can see the beauty even when it is not pretty every day and if you can source your life on the edge of the lake and shout to the silver of the full moon.

It doesn't interest me to know where you live or how much money you have, I want to know if you can get up after a night of grief and despair, weary and bruised to the bone and do what needs to done for the children.

It doesn't interest me to know who you know or how you came to be here, I want to know if you will stand on the center of fire with me and not shrink back.

It doesn't interest me where or what or with whom you have studied, I want to know what sustains you from the inside when all else falls away.

I want to know if you can be alone with yourself and if you truly like the company you keep in the empty moments.

~ Oriah Mountain Dreamer, Indian Elder

The heights by great men reached and kept
Were not attained by sudden flight,
But they, while their companions slept,
Were toiling upward in the night.

~ Henry Wadsworth Longfellow

In Myself

I do not ask for any crown
But that which all may win;
Nor try to conquer any world
Except the one within.

Be thou my guide until I find
Led by a tender hand,
The happy kingdom in myself
And dare to take command.

~ Louisa May Alcott

Lord,
I crawled across the barrenness
To You
With my empty cup,
Uncertain in asking
Any small drop of refreshment.
If only I had known You better,
I'd have come running
With a bucket.

~ Nancy Spiegelberg

Meaning of Service

The Sea of Galilee
and the Dead Sea are
made of the same water.
It flows down,
clear and cool,
from the heights of Hermon
and the roots of
the cedars of Lebanon.
The Sea of Galilee
makes beauty of it,
for the Sea of Galilee
has an outlet. It gets to give.
It gathers in its riches that
it may pour them out again
to fertilize the Jordan plain.
But the Dead Sea with the
same water makes horror.
For the Dead Sea has no outlet.
It gets to keep.

~ Henry Emerson Fosdick

What is Success?

Be To laugh often and much;

To win the respect of intelligent people
and the affection of children;

To earn the appreciation of honest critics
and endure the betrayal of false friends;

To appreciate beauty;

To find the best in others;

To leave the world a bit better, whether by
a healthy child, a garden patch
or a redeemed social condition;

To know even one life has breathed
easier because you have lived;

This is to have succeeded.

- Ralph Waldo Emerson

If I Had My Child To Raise Over Again

If I had my child to raise all over again,
I'd build self-esteem first, and the house later.
I'd finger paint more, and point the finger less.
I would do less correcting and more connecting.

I'd take my eyes off my watch, and watch with my eyes.
I would care to know less and know to care more.
I'd take more hikes and fly more kites.
I'd stop playing serious, and seriously play.

I would run through more fields and gaze at more stars,
I'd do more hugging and less tugging.
I'd see the oak tree in the acorn more often,
I would be firm less often, and affirm much more.

I'd model less about the love of power,
And more about the power of love.

~ Diane Loomans

The Will To Win

If you want a thing bad enough
To go out and fight for it,
Work day and night for it,
Give up your time and your peace and your sleep for it
If only desire of it
Makes you quite mad enough
Never to tire of it,
Makes you hold all other things tawdry and cheap for it
If life seems all empty and useless without it
And all that you scheme and you dream is about it,
If gladly you'll sweat for it,
Fret for it,
Plan for it,
Lose all your terror of God or man for it,
If you'll simply go after that thing that you want,
With all your capacity,
Strength and sagacity,
Faith, hope and confidence, stern pertinacity,
If neither cold poverty, famished and gaunt,
Nor sickness nor pain
Of body or brain
Can turn you away from the thing that you want,
If dogged and grim you besiege and beset it,
You'll get it!

~ Berton Braley

Builder or Wrecker

I watched them tearing a building down,
A gang of men in a busy town.
With a ho-heave-ho and lusty yell,
They swung a beam and a sidewall fell.

I asked the foreman, "Are these men skilled,
The men you'd hire if you had to build?"

He gave me a laugh and said, "No indeed!
Just common labor is all I need.
I can easily wreck in a day or two
What builders have taken a year to do."

And I thought to myself as I went my way,
Which of these two roles have I tried to play?

Am I a builder who works with care,
Measuring life by the rule and square?
Am I shaping my deeds by a well-made plan,
Patiently doing the best I can?

Or am I a wrecker who walks the town,
Content with the labor of tearing down?

~ Author Unknown

The Proof Of Worth

Though victory's proof of the skill you possess,
Defeat is the proof of your grit;
A weakling can smile in his days of success,
But at trouble's first sign he will quit.
So the test of the heart and the test of your pluck
Isn't skies that are sunny and fair,
But how do you stand to the blow that is struck
And how do you battle despair?

A fool can seem wise when the pathway is clear
And it's easy to see the way out,
But the test of man's judgment is something to fear,
And what does he do when in doubt?
And the proof of his faith is the courage he shows
When sorrows lie deep in his breast;
It's the way that he suffers the griefs that he knows
That brings out his worst or his best.

The test of a man is how much he will bear
For a cause which he knows to be right,
How long will he stand in the depths of despair,
How much will he suffer and fight?
There are many to serve when the victory's near
And few are the hurts to be borne,
But it calls for a leader of courage to cheer
The men in a battle forlorn.

It's the way you hold out against odds that are great
That proves what your courage is worth,
It's the way that you stand to the bruises of fate
That shows up your stature and girth.
And victory's nothing but proof of your skill,

Veneered with a glory that's thin,
Unless it is proof of unfaltering will,
And unless you have suffered to win.

~ Edgar Albert Guest

———◄◊►———

How and When

We are often greatly bothered
By two fussy little men,
Who sometimes block our pathway –
Their names are How and When.

If we have a task or duty
Which we can put off a while,
And we do not go and do it –
You should see those two rogues smile!

But there is a way to beat them,
And I will tell you how:
If you have a task or duty,
Do it well, and do it now.

~ Unknown

The Rules of the Game

Life is a game, a journey we're born to play,
With rules that govern every step of the way.
You can choose to win or lose, it's up to you,
Your unique approach is how you break through.

The rules are shrouded in mystery, sometimes unclear,
But one thing's certain: your actions will bring you near
To victory or defeat. The choice is always yours,
But be warned, you cannot defy Universal laws.

Often you may declare you're doing all you can do,
But your results will reveal, that's not entirely true.
For every breach of the rules, you'll pay the price,
And repeat the hard lesson, till you learn it twice.

But don't be discouraged, for every setback's a test,
A chance to learn, to grow, and to do your best.
For only when you've mastered the rules of the game,
Will you emerge victorious, with a life truly yours to claim.

So, play the game of life with intention and might,
Apply the rules with wisdom, and shine with all your light.
For in the end, it's not just about winning or losing the fight,
But about living a life that's authentic, meaningful, and bright.

~ Verusha Robbins

Count That Day Lost

If you sit down at set of sun
And count the acts that you have done,
And, counting, find
One self-denying deed, one word
That eased the heart of him who heard,
One glance most kind
That fell like sunshine where it went-
Then you may count that day well spent.

But if, through all the livelong day,
You've cheered no heart, by yea or nay-
If, through it all
You've nothing done that you can trace
That brought the sunshine to one face-
No act most small
That helped some soul and nothing cost-
Then count that day as worse than lost.

~ George Eliot

The Road Less Travelled

Two roads diverged in a yellow wood,
And sorry I could not travel both
And be one traveler, long I stood
And looked down one as far as I could
To where it bent in the undergrowth;
Then took the other, as just as fair,
And having perhaps the better claim,
Because it was grassy and wanted wear;
Though as for that the passing there
Had worn them really about the same,
And both that morning equally lay
In leaves no step had trodden black.
Oh, I kept the first for another day!
Yet knowing how way leads on to way,
I doubted if I should ever come back.
I shall be telling this with a sigh
Somewhere ages and ages hence:
Two roads diverged in a wood, and I-
I took the one less traveled by,
And that has made all the difference.

~ Robert Frost

Persistence

I must persist if I am to rise.
Life's challenge I see before my eyes,
I set my sights on a worthy task,
That makes me reach beyond my grasp.

Those who persist will often fall,
For a child to walk he first must crawl,
Try he will, till he finds his feet,
He has not yet learnt the word defeat.

Such childish ignorance makes man great,
But learnt too soon, will seal his fate.
When your heart has will, yourself provoke,
From a seed you'll grow to a mighty oak.

~ C.N Andre Day

Serenity Prayer

God, grant me the
Serenity to accept the things I cannot change,
Courage to change the things I can,
And wisdom to know the difference.

~ Reinhold Neibuhr

The Oak tree

A mighty wind blew night and day
It stole the oak tree's leaves away
Then snapped its boughs and pulled its bark
Until the oak was tired and stark

But still the oak tree held its ground
While other trees fell all around
The weary wind gave up and spoke.
How can you still be standing Oak?

The oak tree said, I know that you
Can break each branch of mine in two
Carry every leaf away
Shake my limbs, and make me sway

But I have roots stretched in the earth
Growing stronger since my birth
You'll never touch them, for you see
They are the deepest part of me

Until today, I wasn't sure
Of just how much I could endure
But now I've found, with thanks to you
I'm stronger than I ever knew

~ Johnny Ray Ryder Jr

The Tides Of Providence

It's not what you gather, but what you sow,
That gives the heart a warming glow.
It's not what you get, but what you give,
Decides the kind of life you live.

It's not what you have,
But what you spare.
It's not what you take,
But what you share
That pays the greater dividend
And makes you richer in the end.

It's not what you spend upon yourself
Or hide away upon a shelf,
That brings a blessing for the day.
It's what you scatter by the way.

A wasted effort it may seem.
But what you cast upon the stream
Comes back to you recompense
Upon the tides of providence.

~ Patience Strong

It's Not The Critic Who Counts

It's not the critic who counts,
not the man who points out how the strong man stumbled,
or when the doer of deeds could have done better.

The credit belongs to the man who is actually in the arena;
whose face is marred by dust and sweat and blood;
who strives valiantly;
who errs and comes short again and again;
who knows the great enthusiasms,
the great devotions and spends himself in a worthy cause;
who at the best, knows in the end
the triumph of high achievement;
and who at the worst if he fails,
at least fails while daring greatly,
so that his place shall never be
with those cold and timid souls
who know neither victory nor defeat.

~ Theodore Roosevelt

The Misfits

Here's to the crazy ones.
The misfits.
The rebels.
The troublemakers.
The round pegs in the square holes.
The ones who see things differently.

They're not fond of rules.
And they have no respect for the status quo.
You can praise them, disagree with them, quote them,
disbelieve them, glorify or vilify them.

About the only thing you can't do is ignore them.
Because they change things.
They invent. They imagine. They heal.
They explore. They create. They inspire.
They push the human race forward.

And while some may see them as the crazy ones,
We see genius,
Because the ones who are crazy enough
To think that they can change the world,
Are the ones who do.

~ Steve Jobs (1955-2011), former Apple C.E.O.

Do More

Do more than belong: participate.
Do more than care: help.
Do more than believe: practice.
Do more than be fair: be kind.
Do more than forgive: forget.
Do more than dream: work.

~ William Arthur Ward

There's one sad truth in life I've found
While journeying east and west
The only folks we really wound
Are those we love the best.
We flatter those we scarcely know,
We please the fleeting guest,
And deal full many a thoughtless blow
To those who love us best.

~ Ella Wheeler Wilcox

The Knots Prayer

Dear God:
Please untie the knots
that are in my mind,
my heart and my life.
Remove the have nots,
the can nots and the do nots
that I have in my mind.

Erase the will nots,
may nots,
might nots that may find
a home in my heart.

Release me from the could nots,
would nots and
should nots that obstruct my life.

And most of all,
Dear God,
I ask that you remove from my mind,
my heart and my life all of the 'am nots'
that I have allowed to hold me back,
especially the thought
that I am not good enough.
AMEN

~ Unknown

Beautiful Prayer

I asked God to take away my habit.
God said, No.
It is not for me to take away, but for you to give it up.

I asked God to make my handicapped child whole.
God said, No.
His spirit is whole, his body is only temporary.

I asked God to grant me patience.
God said, No.
Patience is a byproduct of tribulations;
it isn't granted, it is learned.

I asked God to give me happiness.
God said, No.
I give you blessings; Happiness is up to you.

I asked God to spare me pain.
God said, No.
Suffering draws you apart from worldly cares
and brings you closer to me.

I asked God to make my spirit grow.
God said, No.
You must grow on your own,
but I will prune you to make you fruitful.

I asked God for all things that I might enjoy life.
God said, No.
I will give you life, so that you may enjoy all things.

I ask God to help me LOVE others, as much as
He loves me.
God said...Ahhhh, finally you have the idea.

~ Joanne Gobure

Always Remember To Forget

Always remember to forget
The things that made you sad
But never forget to remember
The things that made you glad

Always remember to forget
The friends that proved untrue
But don't forget to remember
Those that have stuck by you

Always remember to forget
The troubles that have passed away
But never, never forget to remember
The blessings that come each day.

~ Unknown

As We Grow Greyer and Greyer

In moments rare, sometimes I dare, to explore thoughts that can cause despair.

Then I feel, life's not fair. We may know we aren't the bodies we wear, but that's what we'll miss, when only one of us is there.

After years of togetherness, after all the love & care, the hand will reach out, and meet only air, on lonely nights, when only one of us is there.

Everyday we'll recall, what he used to say, what she used to wear, the jokes he'd tell, the hearts she'd repair, when the time comes, and only one of us is there.

No gentle peck, no stroking the hair; with the warp gone, will the weft tear, or will it still hold, when only one of us is there?

But,

I have much to do, these thoughts are a snare, to make me just, stand & stare, at what'll be, when only one of us is there.

We have a wonderful life, let's not despair. In the years we have, let's prepare, for when only one of us is there.

Let's make beautiful memories, in the time we share. Let's ask, in our prayer, to remain whole, when only one of us is there.

~ Kishore Asthana (https://sanitybalance.in/)

The Few

The easy roads are crowded,
And the level roads are jammed;
The pleasant little rivers
With the drifting folks are crammed,

But off yonder where it's rocky,
Where you get a better view,
You will find the ranks are thinning
And the travelers are few.

Where the going's smooth and pleasant
You will always find the throng,
For the many, more's the pity,
Seem to like to drift along.

But the steps that call for courage
And the task that's hard to do,
In the end results in glory
For the never-wavering few.

~ Edgar Guest

Keep Your Grit

Hang on! Cling on! No matter what they say;
Push on! Sting on! Things will come your way.

Sitting down and whining never helps a bit.
Best way to get there is by keeping up your grit.

Don't give up hoping when the ship goes down.
Grab a spar or something – just refuse to drown.

Don't think you're dying just because you're hit.
Smile in face of danger and hang to your grit.

Folks die too easy – they sort of fade away;
Make a little error, and give up in dismay.

Kind of man that's needed is the man with ready wit.
To laugh at pain and trouble and keep his grit.

~ Mabel E. Bailey

Forgiveness

If you try to reach inside of your heart
you can find forgiveness, or at least the start
And from that place where you can forgive
is where Hope, and Love, also thrive and live

And with each step that you try to take
and with that chance that your heart might break
Comes so much happiness, and so much strength
which alone can carry you a fantastic length

For hate and anger will not get you there
and though you say that you just don't care
You can EASILY avoid the pain on which hate feeds
. . . the kind of hurt that No one needs

Just make the move, take that first stride
let go of the thing known as "Foolish Pride"
Maybe then you can start to repair the past
into something strong, that will mend, and last!

~ Barry S. Maltese

The Challenge

Let others lead small lives,
But not you.
Let others argue over small things,
But not you.
Let others cry over small hurts,
But not you.
Let others leave their future
In someone else's hands,
But not you.

~ Jim Rohn

Worry is like a distant hill

Worry is like a distant hill
We glimpse against the sky,
We wonder how we ever will
Get up a hill so high.

Yet when we reach the top we see
The roadway left behind
Is not as steep and sheer as we
Have pictured in our mind.

~ Unknown

Attitude

Success is a goal for all mankind,
Achieved through thought and a state of mind,
That strength of purpose we cannot exclude,
For success depends on our attitude.

So hear yourself, your voice within,
It will guide you through your life herein,
Six days of labour, one day of rest,
Shrug not your shoulders, do your best...

Take not in life the mild approach,
The results you receive, you will not boast,
So give your all with plenty of drive,
For none of us leave this world alive.

Labour and learn in pursuit of your dreams,
The best things in life are all upstream,
What you put in, is what you get,
Pain of discipline beats regret.

Life is too long not to do well,
If you do not try, it's a living hell,
So play out your hand, enjoy the ride,
Don't live to regret, for not having tried.

~ C.N. Andre Day

Footprints

One night I dreamed a dream.
I was walking along the beach with my Lord.
Across the dark sky flashed scenes from my life.
For each scene, I noticed two sets of footprints in the sand,
one belonging to me and one to my Lord.

When the last scene of my life shot before me
I looked back at the footprints in the sand.
There was only one set of footprints.
I realized that this was at the lowest and saddest times of my life.
This always bothered me and I questioned the Lord about my
dilemma.

"Lord, You told me when I decided to follow You,
You would walk and talk with me all the way.
But I'm aware that during the most troublesome times of my
life there is only one set of footprints.
I just don't understand why, when I need You most,
You leave me."

He whispered, "My precious child,
I love you and will never leave you,
never, ever, during your trials and testings.
When you saw only one set of footprints,
It was then that I carried you.

~ Unknown

Do It Anyway

People are often unreasonable, irrational, and self-centered.
Forgive them anyway.
If you are kind, people may accuse you of selfish, ulterior
motives.
Be kind anyway.
If you are successful,
you will win some unfaithful friends and some genuine enemies.
Succeed anyway.
If you are honest and sincere people may deceive you.
Be honest and sincere anyway.
What you spend years creating,
others could destroy overnight.
Create anyway.
If you find serenity and happiness, some may be jealous.
Be happy anyway.
The good you do today, will often be forgotten.
Do good anyway.
Give the best you have, and it will never be enough.
Give your best anyway.
In the final analysis, it is between you and God.
It was never between you and them anyway.

~ Mother Teresa

The Burning Dream

I dared to dream a burning dream,
of sounds unheard, of sights unseen;
a drum that tapped a different beat,
a growing flame, a burning.

I dared to stand when others bent.
I dared to go where no-one went.
I raised my head above the crowd,
I took a breath and cried aloud:

"I want to be a better me,
to be the best that I can be.
I want to walk beneath the sun
and do things I've left undone."

I took a step, and then one more.
I spread my wings, prepared to soar.
Some held me back. They thought me mad,
crazy, reckless; maybe bad.

But I kept my eyes upon my dream,
that sound unheard, that sight unseen,
and helping hands reached down for me
to lift me up, to set me free.

New friends saw what I could see;
Said: "Be the best that you can be!
You can do it! We're proud of you!"
So I spread my wings, and then... I FLEW.

~ Unknown

Hugs

It's wondrous what a hug can do.
A hug can cheer you when you're blue.
A hug can say, "I love you so," or
"Gee, I hate to see you go."

A hug is "Welcome back again," and
"Great to see you! Where've you been?"
A hug can soothe a small child's pain,
And bring a rainbow after rain.

The hug! There's just no doubt about it...
We scarcely could survive without it!
A hug delights and warms and charms
It must be why God gave us arms.

Hugs are great for fathers and mothers,
Sweet for sisters, swell for brothers.
And chances are your favorite aunts
Love them more than potted plants.

Kittens crave them; puppies love them;
Heads of state are not above them.
A hug can break the language barrier
And make your travels so much merrier.

No need to fret about your store of 'em;
The more you give, the more there's more of em!
So stretch those arms out without delay,
and give someone a hug today!

~ Unknown

A Priceless Gift

Friendship is a priceless gift
that cannot be bought or sold,
But its value is far greater
than a mountain made of gold.

For gold is cold and lifeless,
it can neither see nor hear
And in the time of trouble
it is powerless to cheer.

It has no ears to listen
nor heart to understand,
It cannot bring you comfort
or reach out a helping hand.

So when you ask God for a gift
Be thankful if He sends
Not diamonds, pearls, or riches
But the love of real true friends.

~ Helen Steiner Rice

Leadership

The leader is best,
When people are hardly aware of his existence,
Not so good when people praise his government,
Less good when people stand in fear,
Worst, when people are contemptuous.
Fail to honor people, and they will fail to honor you.
But of a good leader, who speaks little
When his work is done, his aim fulfilled,
The people say, 'We did it ourselves.'

~ Lao Tzu

Kind hearts are the gardens,
Kind thoughts are the roots,
Kind words are the flowers,
Kind deeds are the fruits.

Take care of your garden
And keep out the weeds,
Fill it with sunshine
Kind words and kind deeds.

~ Henry Wadsworth Longfellow

Judge Gently

Pray don't find fault with the man who limps
or stumbles along the road,
unless you have worn the shoes he wears
or struggled beneath his load.
There may be tacks in his shoes that hurt,
though hidden away from view,
or the burden he bears, placed on your back
might cause you to stumble too.
Don't sneer at the man who's down today
unless you have felt the blow
that caused his fall or felt the shame
that only the fallen know.
You may be strong, but still the blows
that were his if dealt to you,
in the selfsame way, at the selfsame time,
might cause you to stagger too.
Don't be too harsh with the man who sins
or pelt him with word or stone,
unless you are sure, yea, doubly sure,
that you have no sins of your own for
you know perhaps if the tempter's voice
should whisper as softly to you
as it did to him when he went astray,
it might cause you to stumble too.

~ Unknown

Raising Our Children

If we tell our children they're so bad,
They'll grow up as we hope they never had.
But if we tell our children they're so good,
They'll grow up exactly as we hope they would.

If our expectations of them are low,
In their performance it'll show.
But if our expectations of them are high,
They'll stretch and reach for the sky.

If we don't openly show them affection,
It could lead to a misconception.
But if we show them love through touch,
They'll grow close to us.

If with them we hardly talk,
Then at what we say, they'll baulk.
But if with them we'll join and play,
Then, as a family, together we'll stay.

~ Virend Singh

A Big Favour, please!

Dear Reader

Thank you for immersing yourself in the pages of "*100+ Inspirational Poems and Prose About Life and Success.*" I sincerely hope it resonated with you as profoundly as it did with me. Did a specific piece touch your heart, motivate you, or serve as a powerful source of wisdom and inspiration?

Your thoughts on the book are invaluable, especially to others seeking to improve their lives. By sharing your insights in a review, you become a conduit for positive change.

Unfortunately, only a tiny fraction of readers leave reviews. As a self-published author, I don't have the promotional power of a big publishing company. Instead, I rely on valued readers like you to spread the word about the potential impact of the life lessons woven into these concise poems and anecdotes.

Imagine *your words* igniting inspiration in someone else's life. By leaving a review, you're doing just that, and helping create a ripple effect of transformation that can touch countless other lives. Here's how you can make a difference:

1. Go to Amazon or www.Chosen4u.com/vra/
2. Select "100+ Inspirational Poems and Prose About Life and Success."
3. Scroll down to "Customer reviews," click "Write a customer review," and share your honest thoughts

Your review doesn't need to be lengthy; it just needs to reflect your truth.

Thank you for being part of this meaningful journey!

With heartfelt gratitude,
Verusha Robbins

P.S. If these poems and prose have made you eager to probe further into life's lessons, you'll love "*100+ Inspirational Short Stories about Success and Happiness.*" It's just as inspiring!

Our Gift To You

If you enjoyed this book, then you will find the following FREE resources just as enlightening:

- The 10 Best Motivational Stories to Uplift and Inspire
- The Fastest Road to Success – The Secret Used by the World's Richest People to Double, Triple or Even 10X Their Income and Wealth
- My Journey to a Better Me – a short 12-module online course comprising a guide, printable journal and monthly planner for each module.

Go to www.Chosen4U.com/GiftsPP/ to access your free resources now.

Acknowledgements

This book's collection of poems and anecdotes has been gathered over two decades and sourced from various mediums, including emails, newsletters, online publications, and audio recordings. As with any anthology of quotations, tracing the origins of certain materials has presented challenges. While we have made every reasonable effort to attribute sources where possible, some have unfortunately remained obscure. We sincerely appreciate all those whose narratives have contributed to this work, even where precise citation has proven elusive.

Other resources by Verusha & Virend

Ready to go beyond the 100+ inspirational stories you just read?

The Inexplicable Laws of Success: Discover the Hidden Truths that Separate the 'Best' from the 'Rest' delves deeper, transforming those sparks of inspiration into a proven roadmap for achieving your dreams.

This groundbreaking book unveils the hidden truths that separate the consistently successful from the rest. It's not about magic formulas - it's about harnessing the power within you and aligning yourself with the universal principles that govern success.

Don't just be inspired, be empowered. Embark on a transformative journey with *The Inexplicable Laws of Success*. Your best self is waiting! Download for <u>free</u> from leading <u>online bookstores</u>.

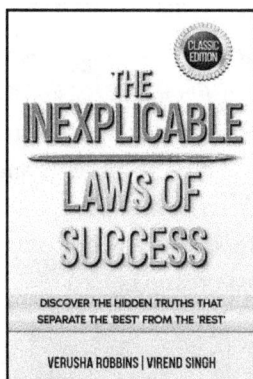

PROFESSIONAL ENDORSEMENTS:

"This book gives ideas and insights into unlocking and releasing your full potential for happiness and success."

- Brian Tracy, International Best-Selling Author

100+ Inspirational Short Stories about Success and Happiness: Insightful Words of Wisdom to Motivate, Educate and Create A More Empowered You. Everyone, at some point in their lives, feels overwhelmed by the challenges and obstacles that they have to face. In times of difficulty, we often look around to find a source of inspiration and hope. Sometimes the easiest and most powerful way to get a message across is through a story. Stories hold our attention and stay with us long after we have heard them. *100+ Inspirational Short Stories about Success and Happiness* will inspire and uplift readers with its stories of optimism, faith, and strength.

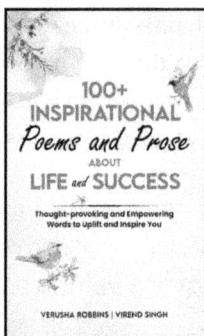

Inspirational Words and Positive Quotes to Live By: An Insightful Collection of Motivational Quotes is packed with wisdom and serve to remind you that life can be good, no matter what challenges you may be facing. These quotes will empower and encourage you to live your life to the fullest. They come from accomplished people, sages, philosophers and thinkers, all of whom started out as an ordinary citizen and have achieved greatness.

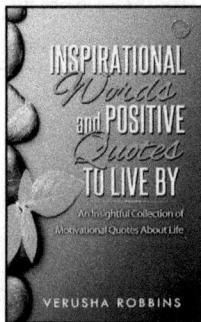

About The Authors

This book is the collaborative effort of Virend and Verusha, a father-daughter team.

Verusha Robbins is an accomplished writer and entrepreneur who thrives at both, captivating audiences with fictional narratives that entertain, as well as empowering others through personal transformation. Her expertise in Media & Writing and Editing & Publishing fuels her success in both realms. Her professional journey includes pivotal roles at esteemed publishing companies like Hay House (Australia). Looking ahead, Verusha remains committed to weaving captivating worlds through fiction while equipping readers with the knowledge they need to flourish in all aspects of life.

Virend Singh, a seasoned entrepreneur with an MBA, leverages his years of experience to empower others. His journey, marked by both triumphs and challenges, has instilled in him a deep understanding of the mindset and behaviors that drive high achievers. Drawing on these firsthand insights, Virend collaborates with his daughter, Verusha, in a unique father-daughter team. Together, they empower individuals to unlock their full potential, achieving success in both personal and professional realms.

For fans of fantasy...

If you are drawn to fantasy, in particular dark romance fantasy, then you will truly enjoy Verusha's latest novels:

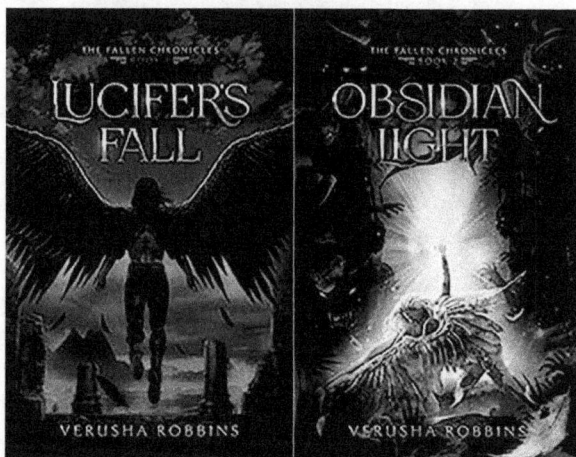

If you love the intricate world-building in Sarah J. Maas, Carissa Broadbent, and Anne Bishop's works, prepare to be mesmerized by these books.

Step into a spellbinding realm where angels and demons clash in an epic saga. Sandriel, a fallen angel with a mysterious past, is ensnared in a perilous dance with Lucifer, the most mesmerizing fallen angel of all. Her mission is clear: rescue the captive warrior angels in Hell and combat the Fallen, all while resisting the overwhelming allure of the Devil himself.

Themes to Captivate You:

- Enemies to Lovers
- Hell and Angels

- Captivity and Liberation
- Greek Mythology
- Emotional Healing and Scars
- Revenge and Redemption

Prepare for an exhilarating journey brimming with multifaceted characters, forbidden love, and jaw-dropping twists that will keep you reading late into the night.

Readers are enthralled by "Lucifer's Fall" and "Obsidian Light":

- "A masterpiece of storytelling. I couldn't put it down!"
- "The twists and turns are mind-blowing!"
- "I haven't been this captivated by a book in years!"
- "This book is 'unputdownable,' unique, and mysteriously beautiful."

Free Sample Available!

Download the first six chapters of "Lucifer's Fall" for free and discover why readers can't get enough. Visit www.chosen4u.com/LF6

Available now on all major platforms.

**For more resources by
Verusha and Virend
go to**

www.inkNivory.com/resources/

and

www.CoolSelfHelpTips.com

www.ingramcontent.com/pod-product-compliance
Lightning Source LLC
Chambersburg PA
CBHW060119050426
42448CB00010B/1936